FEB 2 8 2006

Nursery Rhymes
and
Nursery Songs

Ernest Griset.

Nursery Rhymes
and
Nursery Songs

Set to Original Music by

J. W. ELLIOTT

WITH ILLUSTRATIONS ENGRAVED
BY THE BROTHERS DALZIEL

DOVER PUBLICATIONS, INC.
Mineola, New York

Bibliographical Note

This Dover edition, first published in 2004, is an unabridged reprint of *National Nursery Rhymes and Nursery Songs,* published by Novello and Company, Limited, London, n.d. [1870].

International Standard Book Number: 0-486-43806-6

Manufactured in the United States of America
Dover Publications, Inc., 31 East 2nd Street, Mineola, N.Y. 11501

PREFACE.

THE present volume is intended as a contribution to what may be justly considered a not unimportant department of our national song literature — the Nursery Rhymes namely, which seem appointed, by tacit and universal consent, to be "said or sung," and to be listened to, with unwearied interest and appreciation, in those great National Institutions the British Nursery and Home School-room. To all who are interested in the selection of books for children the book is now offered by the Publishers, with the hope that it may gain general and extended approbation. Especial pains have been taken to secure the suffrage of that still larger public, in petticoats and knicker-bockers, whom a genial English writer of the last century, who loved children, and spoke and wrote of them with infinite tenderness and affection, describes as "masters in all the learning on the other side of eight years old."

If it be true—as asserted by one of the greatest of English critics and authors—that Sir Roger de Coverley and Mr. Spectator are more real than nine-tenths of the heroes of the last century, and that almost the only autobiography to be received entirely without distrust and disbelief is that of one ROBINSON CRUSOE, Mariner, of York—then surely those important personages, JACK and JILL, HUMPTY DUMPTY, and my LADY WIND, are real and distinct entities in the mind of every little child whose nursery education has not been entirely and unwarrantably neglected ; and therefore it has seemed good to the Publishers to present to the children of the present day the adventures of those heroes, embellished with whatever pictorial illustration, careful selection, musical accompaniment, and the advantages of artistic typography and detail can contribute, to render them more acceptable to all English children.

In the arrangement of the musical portion of the volume, especial care has been taken by MR. ELLIOTT to keep the songs strictly within the capacity of children's execution, and the compass of children's voices. In his own family he has found a young jury ready to test the various tunes, and has composed only such melodies as were likely to meet with prompt acceptance, and be easily remembered.

The pictorial illustrations of the book have been designed under the superintendence of, and engraved by, the BROTHERS DALZIEL.

Among the old favourites a few new aspirants to popularity will be found ; but it is hoped that their presence will be considered an additional attraction. and in no way lessen the pretensions of the present volume to be considered a compendium of National Nursery Rhymes.

CONTENTS.

CONTENTS.

* Words by M. L. ELLIOTT.

THE ILLUSTRATIONS ENGRAVED BY THE BROTHERS DALZIEL.

Nursery Rhymes
and
Nursery Songs

Mistress Mary.

Allegretto moderato.

Mis-tress Ma - ry, quite con - tra - ry, How does your gar-den grow? With

cock - le - shells, and sil - ver bells, And fair maids all in a row.

Jack and Jill.

Jack and Jill Went up the hill, To fetch a pail of wa - ter;

Jack fell down, And broke his crown, And Jill came tum - bling af - ter.

JACK AND JILL

Second Verse.

Up Jack got, And home did trot, As fast as he could ca - per;

Went to bed, To mend his head, With vi - ne-gar and brown pa - per.

Third Verse.

Jill came in, And she did grin, To see his pa - per plais - ter.

Mo-ther, vex'd, Did whip her next, For caus - ing Jack's dis - as - ter.

Twinkle, twinkle, little star.

Twin-kle, twin-kle, lit-tle star, How I won-der what you are! Up a-bove the world so high, Like a dia-mond in the sky.

TWINKLE, TWINKLE, LITTLE STAR.

Baa, Baa, Black Sheep.

Andante.

Baa, Baa, Black Sheep, Have you a - ny wool? Yes sir, yes sir, Three bags full;

cres. poco lento   *rallentando e dim.*

One for my Master, One for my Dame, But none for the little boy Who cries in the lane.

Dickory, dickory, dock.

Dick-o-ry, dick-o-ry, dock; The

mouse ran up the clock; The

clock struck One, The mouse ran down;

Dick-o-ry, dick-o-ry, dock.

Ding, Dong, Bell.

Ding, dong, bell, Pus - sy's in the well; Who put her in?

Lit - tle John - ny Green; Who pull'd her out? Lit - tle Tommy Trout. What a

naugh - ty boy was that, To drown poor Pus - sy - Cat.

Pussy-Cat, Pussy-Cat.

Pussy-cat, pussy-cat, where have you been? I've been to London to visit the Queen.

Pussy-cat, pussy-cat, what did you there? I frighten'd a lit-tle mouse under her chair.

Nineteen Birds.

Moderato e marcato.

Nineteen birds and one bird more, Just make twen-ty, and that's a score.

SECOND VERSE.

To the score then add but one; That will make just twen - ty - one.

3. Now add two, and you will see
   You have made up twenty-three.

4. If you like these clever tricks,
   Add three more for twenty-six.

5. Then three more, if you have time:
   Now you've got to twenty-nine.

6. Twenty-nine now quickly take—
   Add one more and Thirty make

The Child and the Star.

Andante con moto e tranquillo.

1. Little star that shines so bright, Come and peep at me to-night, For I
2. Little star! O tell me, pray, Where you hide yourself all day? Have you

of-ten watch for you In the pret-ty sky so blue.
got a home like me, And a fa-ther kind to see?

3. Little Child! at you I peep
   While you lie so fast asleep;
   But when morn begins to break,
   I my homeward journey take.

4. For I've many friends on high,
   Living with me in the sky;
   And a loving Father, too,
   Who commands what I'm to do

(11)

I had a little Doggy.

Andante non troppo.

I had a lit-tle dog-gy that used to sit and beg, But

Doggy tumbled down the stairs, and broke his lit-tle leg; Oh! Doggy, I will nurse you, and

I HAD A LITTLE DOGGY.

try to make you well; And you shall have a collar with a pret-ty lit-tle bell.

SECOND AND THIRD VERSES.

Ah! Dog-gy, don't you think you should ve - ry faith-ful be, For
But, Dog-gy, you must pro - mise (and mind your word you keep) Not

hav-ing such a lov-ing friend to comfort you as me. And when your leg is bet-ter, and
once to teaze the lit-tle lambs, or run among the sheep. And then the yel-low "chicks," that

you can run and play, We'll have a scamper in the fields, and see them making hay.
play up-on the grass, You must not e-ven wag your tail to scare them as you pass.

Little Bo-Peep.

Andante quasi Allegretto.

Lit-tle Bo-Peep has lost her sheep, And can't tell where to find them;

Leave them a-lone, and they'll come home, Wagging their tails be - hind them.

LITTLE BO-PEEP.

Dolly and her Mamma.

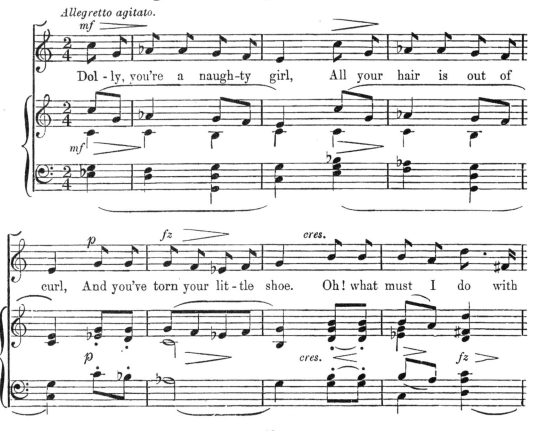

Dol - ly, you're a naugh-ty girl, All your hair is out of curl, And you've torn your lit - tle shoe. Oh! what must I do with

DOLLY AND HER MAMMA.

you? You shall on-ly have dry bread, Dol-ly, you shall go to bed.

SECOND AND THIRD VERSES.

Do you hear, Miss, what I say? Are you go-ing to o-
But I mean to try and grow All Mam-ma can wish, you

-bey? That's what Mo-ther says to me, So I know it's right, you
know; Ne-ver in-to pas-sions fly, Or, when thwarted, sulk and

see; For some-times *I'm* naughty, too, Dol-ly, dear, as well as **you.**
cry. So, my Dol-ly, you must be Good and gen-tle, just like **me.**

Ride a Cock-horse to Banbury Cross.

Ride a Cock-horse to Ban-bu-ry Cross, To see a fine la-dy up-on a white horse,

R'ngs on her fingers, and bells on her toes, She shall have mu-sic wher-e-ver she goes.

Little maid, pretty maid.

'Lit-tle maid, pret-ty maid, Whither goest thou?' 'Down in the meadow to milk my cow.'

'Shall I go with thee?' 'No, not now; When I send for thee, then come thou.'

Whittington for ever.

Moderato.
Time well marked.

mf

Whit - ting- ton for e - ver, Hur - rah! Hur - rah! Hur - rah!

mf   ten.

WHITTINGTON FOR EVER.

Lord Mayor of Lon - don, Hur - rah! Hur-rah! Hur-rah! Hur - -rah! Hur-rah! Hur - rah! Hur - rah! Hur - rah! Hur - rah! Hur - -rah! Hur-rah! Hur-rah! Whit-ting-ton for e - ver, Lord Mayor of London, Hur - - rah! Hur - rah! Hur - rah! Hur-rah! Hur-rah! Hur - rah!

Little Jack Horner.

Allegretto con moto.

Little Jack Hor-ner Sat in a cor - ner, Eating a Christ-mas pie; He

put in his thumb, And pull'd out a plum, And said, "What a good boy am I!"

Tom, the Piper's Son.

Allegretto e marcato.

Tom, Tom, the pi-per's son, Stole a pig, and a-way he run! The

pig was eat, And Tom was beat, Which sent him howling down the street.

See-saw, Margery Daw.

See - saw, Mar-ge-ry Daw, Jack shall have a new mas - ter,

He shall have but a pen-ny a day, Be-cause he wont work a-ny fast - er.

Allegretto.
mf
cres. e ritard.

(24)

A, B, C, tumble down D.

A, B, C, tum-ble down D, The cat's in the cupboard and can't see me.

Goosey, goosey gander.

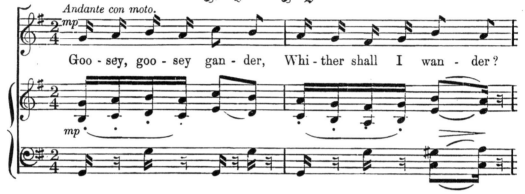

Andante con moto.

Goo - sey, goo - sey gan - der, Whi - ther shall I wan - der?

Up stairs and down stairs, And in my la-dy's chamber; There I met an old man, Who

would not say his prayers; I took him by the left leg, And threw him down the stairs.

Little jumping Joan.

Here am I, lit - tle jump - ing Joan; When

no - bo - dy's with me, I'm al - ways a - lone.

There was a Crooked Man.

Allegretto moderato.

There was a crook-ed man, and he went a crook-ed mile, He

found a crook-ed sixpence up - on a crook-ed stile: He bought a crook-ed cat, which

caught a crooked mouse, And they all liv'd to-gether in a crooked lit-tle house.

Poor Dog Bright.

Poor Dog Bright, Ran off with all his might, Be-cause the Cat was af-ter him, Poor Dog Bright.

Poor Cat Fright, Ran off with all her might, Be-cause the Dog was af-ter her, Poor Cat Fright.

Humpty Dumpty.

Allegretto.

Hump - ty Dump - ty, sat on a wall, Hump - ty Dump - ty

had a great fall: All the king's horses, and all the king's men,

Could-n't put Hump - ty Dump - ty to - ge - - ther a - gain.

Simple Simon.

Allegro moderato.

1. Sim - ple Si - mon met a pie-man Go - ing to the fair; Says
2. Says the man to Sim - ple Si-mon, "Do you mean to pay?" Says

Sim - ple Si - mon to the pie - man, "Let me taste your ware."
Si - mon, "Yes, of course I do," And then he ran a - way!

Sing a Song of Sixpence.

Sing a Song of Six-pence, A pock-et full of Rye;

Four-and-twen-ty Blackbirds Bak'd in a Pie. When the Pie was o-pen'd, The

SING A SONG OF SIXPENCE.

(33)

The Nurse's Song.

Allegretto moderato.

1. Dance a ba - by, did - dy; What can Mammy do wid 'e?..
2. Smile, my ba - by bon - ny; What will time bring on 'e?..

Sit in a lap, Give it some pap, And dance a ba - by did - dy...
Sor-row and care, Frowns and grey hair; So smile, my ba - by bon - ny...

THE NURSE'S SONG.

Third Verse.

mp

Laugh, my ba - by, beau - ty; . . What will time do to ye ? .

Furrow your cheek, Wrinkle your neck; So laugh, my ba - by, beau - ty . . .

Fourth Verse.

mp

Dance, my ba - by, dear - y ; . . . Mother will never be wea - ry . . .

Fro - lic and play, Now while you may; So dance, my ba - by, dear - y . . .

(35)

Six little Snails.

Allegretto e marcato.

Six lit - tle Snails Liv'd in a tree,

John - ny threw a big stone, Down came three.

The King of France.

The King of France, and four thou-sand men, Drew their swords, and put them up a-gain.

My Lady Wind.

1. My la - dy wind, my la - dy wind, Went round a - bout the house to find A
2. And then one night, when it was dark, She blew up such a ti - ny spark That

chink to get her foot in, her foot in; She tried the key-hole in the door, She
all the house was pother'd, was po - ther'd: From it she rais'd up such a flame, As

MY LADY WIND.

tried the cre-vice in the floor, And drove the chim-ney soot in, the soot in.
flam'd a-way to Belt-ing Lane, And White Cross folks were smother'd, were smo - ther'd.

THIRD VERSE.

And thus when once, my lit - tle dears, A whis-per reach - es itch - ing ears, The

same will come, you'll find, you'll find; . . . Take my ad-vice, restrain the tongue, Re -

- mem-ber what old Nurse has sung Of bu - sy la - dy wind, la - dy wind. . .

The Feast of Lanterns.

Allegretto e marcato.

Tching - a - ring - a - ring - tching, Feast of Lan - terns,

What a lot of chop-sticks, bombs and gongs; Four-and-twen - ty thou-sand

crink- um-crank-ums, All a-mong the bells and the ding - dongs.

Is John Smith within?

Andante con moto.

Is John Smith within?—Yes, that he is. Can he set a shoe?--Ay, mar-ry, two,

Here a nail, there a nail, Tick tack, too, Here a nail, there a nail, Tick, tack, too.

When the snow is on the ground.

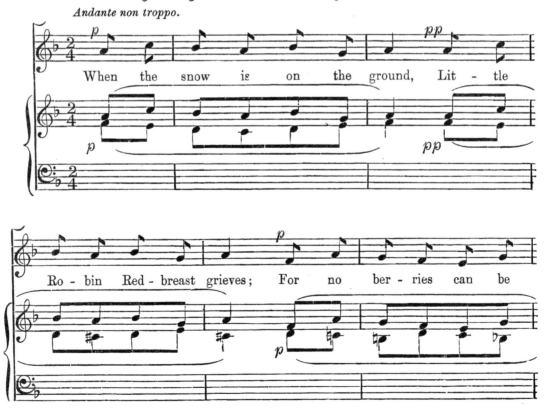

Andante non troppo.

When the snow is on the ground, Lit - tle Ro - bin Red - breast grieves; For no ber - ries can be

WHEN THE SNOW IS ON THE GROUND.

found, And on the trees there are no leaves. The air is cold, the worms are hid, For this poor bird what can be done? We'll strew him here some crumbs of bread, And then he'll live till the snow is gone.

Three little mice.

Three lit-tle mice crept out to see What they could find to have for tea (For

they were dain - ty, sau - cy mice, And lik'd to nib- ble something nice), But

THREE LITTLE MICE.

Pussy's eyes, so big and bright, Soon sent them scampering off in a fright.

Second Verse.

Three Tabby Cats went forth to mouse, And said, "Let's have a gay carouse." For

they were handsome, ac - tive cats, And famed for catching mice and rats. But

savage dogs, disposed to bite. These cats declined to encounter in fight.

Little Tommy Tucker.

Lit - tle Tom - my Tuck - er, Sing for your sup - per.

What shall he sing for? White bread and but - ter. How can he cut it With -

- out a - ny knife? How can he mar - ry With - out a - ny wife?

The North wind doth blow.

The North wind doth blow, And we shall have snow, And
What will poor Ro - bin do then? He'll sit in the barn, And
keep him - self warm, And tuck his head un - der his wing. Poor thing!

The Man in the Moon.

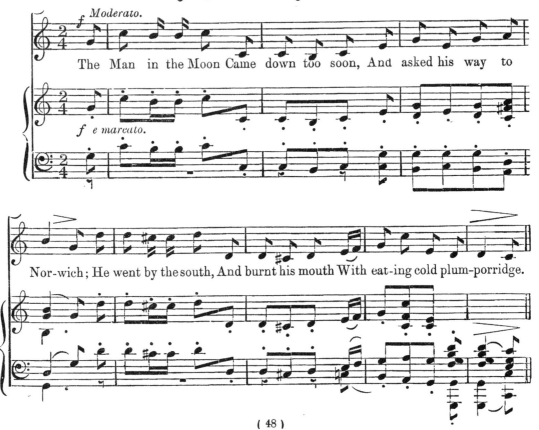

Moderato.

The Man in the Moon Came down too soon, And asked his way to Nor-wich; He went by the south, And burnt his mouth With eat-ing cold plum-porridge.

Taffy was a Welshman.

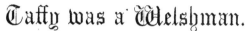

Allegretto.

Taf - fy was a Welsh-man, Taf - fy was a thief,

Taf- fy came to my house, And stole a piece of beef. Then I went to his house,

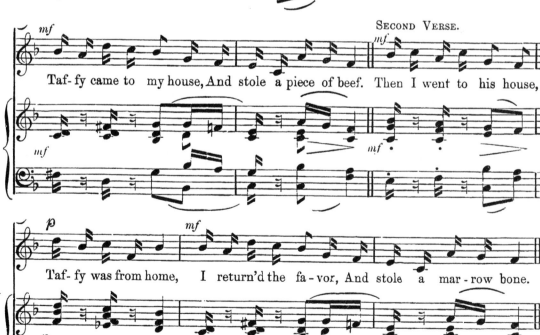

SECOND VERSE.

Taf- fy was from home, I return'd the fa - vor, And stole a mar - row bone.

(49)

Hey, diddle diddle.

Allegro.

Hey, diddle, diddle, The cat and the fiddle, The cow jump'd o-ver the moon; The

lit-tle dog laughed To see such sport, And the dish ran af-ter the spoon.

I love little Pussy.

Andante non troppo.
With tenderness.

I love lit - tle Pus - sy, her coat is so warm, And
if I don't hurt her, she'll do me no harm. I'll sit by the fire and
give her some food, And Pus - sy will love me, be - cause I am good.

The Old Man Clothed in Leather.

One mist - y, moist - y morn - ing, When cloud - y was the wea - ther, O there I met an old man cloth-ed all in lea - ther,

Cloth-ed all in lea - ther, With cap un -der his chin, O how d'ye do? and

THE OLD MAN CLOTHED IN LEATHER.

how d'ye do? And how d'ye do, a - gain? I shook his hand at

part - ing, Tho' cloud - y was the wea - ther, This im - be - cile old "par - ty,"

Cloth - ed all in lea - ther, Cloth - ed all in lea - ther, With cap un - der his

chin: O fare - thee - well, and fare - thee - well, And fare - thee - well a - gain.

Curly Locks!

Cur - ly locks! cur - ly locks! wilt thou be mine? Thou

shalt not wash dish - es nor yet feed the swine; But sit on a cushion, and

sew a fine seam, And feast up - on straw-ber-ries, su - gar, and cream.

The Lazy Cat.

Allegretto.

Pus - sy, where have you been to day? In the meadows a-sleep in the hay.

Pus - sy, you are a la - zy Cat, If you have done no more than that.

Three Children Sliding.

Three chil-dren sli - ding on the ice, All on a sum-mer's day, As it fell out they all fell in, The rest they ran a - way.

May be sung as a Four-part Song

THREE CHILDREN SLIDING.

(57)

The Jolly Tester.

Oh, my lit-tle six-pence, my pret-ty lit-tle six-pence,

I love six-pence bet-ter than my life; I spent a pen-ny of it, I

THE JOLLY TESTER.

THE JOLLY TESTER.

Fourth Verse.

Oh, my lit - tle no - thing, my pret - ty lit - tle no - thing:

What will no - thing buy for my wife? I have no - thing,

I spend no - thing, I love no - thing bet - ter than my wife.

Georgie Porgie.

Georgie Porgie, pudding and pie, Kiss'd the girls and made them cry:

When the girls came out to play, Georgie Porgie ran away.

The Three Crows.

Three Crows there were once who sat on a stone, Fal la la la la.... But two flew a-way, and

THE THREE CROWS.

then there was one. Fal la la la la la. . . . The

o- ther Crow felt so ti - mid a-lone, Fal la la la la la, . . . That

he flew a - way, and then there was none. Fal la la la la la. . .

A Little Cock-sparrow.

Allegretto scherzando.

A lit - tle cock spar - row sat

on a green tree, And he chirrup'd and chirrup'd, so

merry was he, But a naughty boy came with a

A LITTLE COCK SPARROW.

Second Verse.

small bow and arrow, De - ter - min'd to shoot this lit - tle cock spar - row.

"This lit-tle cock sparrow shall make me a stew," Said this naughty boy, "Yes, and a

lit -tle pie, too." "Oh! no," said the sparrow, "I won't make a stew," So he

flutter'd his wings and a - way he flew.

Maggie's Pet.

1. Sweet Mag - gie had a lit - tle bird, And "Gol - die" was his
2. A lump of su - gar sweet and white, Would Mag - gie give her

name, And on her hand he used to sit, He was so ve - ry
Dick, And then she'd watch how ea - ger - ly He'd fly to it and

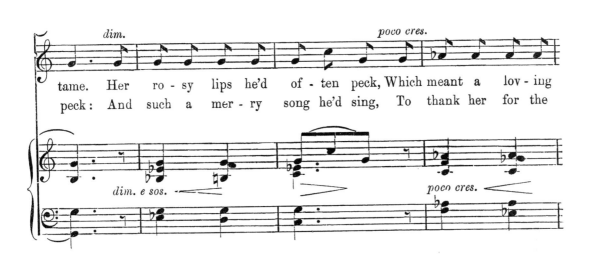

tame. Her ro - sy lips he'd of - ten peck, Which meant a lov - ing
peck: And such a mer - ry song he'd sing, To thank her for the

kiss. Oh! would not you de - light to have A pret - ty bird like this.
treat, For lit - tle birds (like lit - tle girls) Love something nice to eat.

MAGGIE'S PET.

THIRD VERSE.

A - las! one day a hun-gry cat, With ve - ry spite - ful eyes. Be - held poor "Gol-die's" o - pen cage, Oh! what a glad sur - prise! So mew - ing loud with cru - el glee, She spread her wick - ed claws, And soon the ten-der lit - tle bird was fix'd with-in her jaws.

MAGGIE'S PET.

Fourth Verse.

I do not care to tell how much Our dar-ling Mag-gie cried, Or how she kiss'd the emp-ty cage The day poor bir-die died; One lit-tle gold-en fea-ther, soft, I know she trea-sures yet, 'Twas all the cru-el, spite-ful cat, Did leave of Maggie's pet.

THE DEATH AND BURIAL OF COCK ROBIN.

The Death and Burial of Cock Robin.

THE DEATH AND BURIAL OF COCK ROBIN.

I caught his blood." Who'll make his shroud? "I," said the Bee-tle; "With my thread and nee-dle I'll make his shroud." Who'll bear the torch?

"I," said the Lin-net, "Will come in a mi-nute; I'll bear the torch." Who'll be the clerk? "I," said the Lark,

THE DEATH AND BURIAL OF COCK ROBIN.

THE DEATH AND BURIAL OF COCK ROBIN.

Who'll be chief mourn-er? "I," said the Dove; "I mourn for my love,

I'll be chief mourn-er." Who'll sing his dirge? "I," said the

Thrush; "As I sing in a bush, I'll sing his dirge."

Who'll car-ry his cof-fin? "I," said the Kite; "If it be in the

THE DEATH AND BURIAL OF COCK ROBIN.

night, I'll car - ry his cof - fin." Who'll toll the bell?

"I," said the Bull; "Be - cause I can pull, I'll toll the bell."

All the birds of the air Fell sigh - ing and sob - bing, When they

heard the bell toll For poor Cock Ro - bin.

Lullaby.

LULLABY.

When lit - tle Bir - die bye-bye goes, Qui - et as mice in church - es, He puts his head where no one knows, On one leg he perch - es. When lit - tle Ba - bie bye-bye goes, On Mamma's arm re - pos - ing; Soon he lies be -

sostenuto.   dim. e ritard.

cres.

pp legato e ben sostenuto.

poco cres.

LULLABY.

-neath the clothes, Safe in the cra - dle do - zing.

When pret-ty Pus - sy goes to sleep, Tail and nose to - ge - ther,

Then lit-tle mice a - round her creep, Light-ly as a fea - ther.

(78)

LULLABY.

When lit-tle Ba - bie goes to sleep, .. And he is ve -ry near us,

pp legato e ben sostenuto.

Then on tip - toe soft - ly creep, That Ba - bie may not hear us.

Lul-la-by! Lul-la-by! .... Lulla, Lul - la, Lul - la - by! ...

MOTHER TABBYSKINS.

Mother Tabbyskins.

(The Words are printed by the kind permission of Messrs. Strahan & Co.)

MOTHER TABBYSKINS.

Kit-tens in the gar-den, Looking in her face, Learning how to spit and swear,

Oh, what a dis-grace! Ve-ry wrong, ve-ry wrong, Ve-ry wrong, and bad;

Such a sub-ject for our song, Makes us all too sad. Old Mother Tab-by-skins,

Stick-ing out her head, Gave a howl, and then a yowl, Hobbled off to bed.

MOTHER TABBYSKINS.

Ve - ry sick, ve - ry sick, Ve - ry sa - vage, too; Pray send for a doc-tor quick—

A - ny one will do!

Doc-tor mouse came creeping, Creeping to her bed; Lanc'd her gums and felt her pulse,

Whis-per'd she was dead. Ve - ry sly, ve - ry sly, The *real* old cat

MOTHER TABBYSKINS.

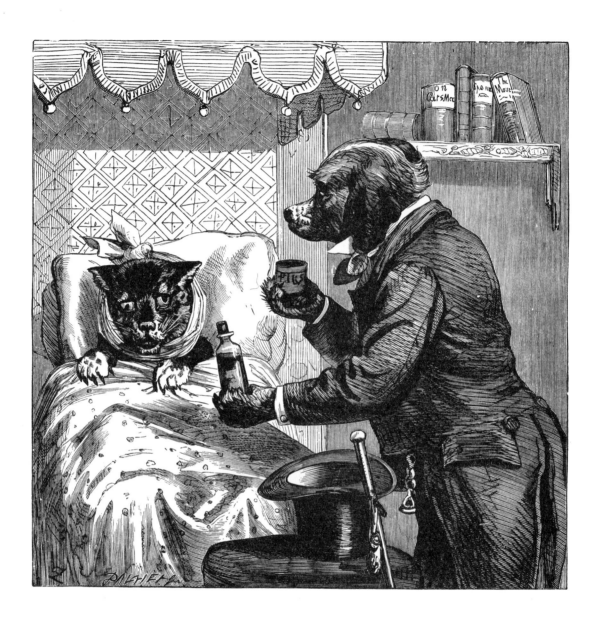

"Dear Mother Tab-byskins, And how are you now? Let me feel your pulse?—so, so:

MOTHER TABBYSKINS.

MOTHER TABBYSKINS.

Lit-tle doc-tor he, But for Doc-tor Dog's ad-vice *You* must pay the fee.

Doc-tor Dog comes near-er,

Says she must be bled; I heard Mo-ther Tab-by-skins Screaming in her bed.

Ve-ry near, ve-ry near, Scuffling out and in; Doc-tor Dog looks full and queer—

MOTHER TABBYSKINS.

Where is Tab-by-skin? I will tell the Mo-ral With-out a-ny fuss?

Those who lead the young a-stray, *Al-ways* suf-fer thus. Ve-ry nice, ve-ry nice,

Let our conduct be; For all doc-tors are not mice, Some are dogs, you see!

THE SPIDER AND THE FLY.

The Spider and the Fly.

(A NURSERY DITTY.)

see so ma-ny curious things you never saw before, Will you, will you, will you

walk in, pret-ty fly? Will you, will you, will you walk in, pret-ty fly? . . .

. . . . pret-ty fly, pret-ty fly?"

"My fine house is al-ways o-pen," said the Spider to the Fly, "I'm

THE SPIDER AND THE FLY.

glad to have the company of all I see go by;" "They go

in but dont come out again—I've heard of you before." "Oh yes, they do, I always let them

out at my back door, Will you, will you, will you walk in, pret-ty fly? Will you

will you, will you walk in, pret-ty fly? . . . . pret-ty fly, pret-ty

(93)

THE SPIDER AND THE FLY.

fly?" . . . . "Will you

grant me one sweet kiss, dear," says the Spider to the Fly, "To taste your charming lips, I've a

cu-ri-o-si-ty." Says the Fly, "If once our lips did meet, a

wager I would lay, Of ten to one you would not af-ter let them come a-way." "Will you

will you,   will you, walk in, pret-ty fly? Will you,   will you,   will you

walk in pret-ty fly? .... pret-ty fly,   pret-ty   fly?" .... .

"If not kiss, will you shake hands, then?" says the

Spider to the Fly, "Be-fore you leave me to myself, with sor-row sad to sigh."

Says the Fly, "there's nothing so at-trac-tive un-to you be-longs; I de-
clare you should not touch me, e-ven with a pair of tongs,' 'Will you, will you, will you,
walk in, pret-ty fly? Will you, will you, will you walk in, pret-ty fly? . . .
. . . pret-ty fly, pret-ty fly?" . . . . .

THE SPIDER AND THE FLY.

"Oh, what handsome wings you've got," says the Spider to the Fly, "If I had on-ly such a pair, I in the air would fly; But 'tis use-less my re-pi-ning, and on-ly i-dle talk, You can fly up in the air, while I'm o-bliged to walk. Will you, will you, will you walk in, pret-ty fly? Will you,

THE SPIDER AND THE FLY.

Ernes. Griset.

in the web caught fast; The Spider laugh'd, "Ah, ah, my boy, I have you safe at last. Will you,

will you, will you, will you, walk *out*, pret-ty fly? Will you, will you, will you

THE SPIDER AND THE FLY.

walk *out*, pret-ty fly? ..... pret-ty fly, pret-ty fly?" . . . .

"Tell me, pray, how are you now?" says the

Spider to the Fly, "You fools will ne-ver wisdom get, un - less you dear-ly buy;

'Tis va - ni-ty that ever makes re - pentance come too late, And

(100)

you who in - to cobwebs run, right well deserve your fate, Listen, lis-ten, lis-ten,

fool-ish lit - tle Fly, Listen, listen to me, foolish, fool-ish lit - tle Fly; . . . .

. . . . lit -tle fly, lit - tle fly?"

So now all young folks take warning by this foolish lit-tle fly, The

Spider's name is "*Pleasure*," to catch you he will try; For al-

- though you may think my ad - vice is quite a bore, You're lost if you stand parleying out-

- side of "*Pleasure's*" door, Re - member, remember, the fool-ish lit - tle fly, Re -

- mem - ber, Oh! re - mem - ber, the fool - ish lit - tle Fly. . . . .

The Thievish Mouse.

A sto - ry sad I've got to tell a - bout a lit - tle

mouse With bright brown eyes, Who used to scam - per up and down the

THE THIEVISH MOUSE.

house: No cheese was safe, no Birth - day cake, on ei - ther shelf or

ground, For Mouse would sure - ly find it out, and nib - ble it all round.

I can - not tell you how each night this naugh - ty Mouse would

roam, Her lit - tle nose thrust in - to things she should have left a -

THE THIEVISH MOUSE.

- lone: It mat-ter'd not where they were put, in cup-board or on

shelf, This cunning Mouse would "sniff" them out, And cool-ly help her - self.

Aunt Ma - ry said, "It is no use to hide the cakes and

pies, For some-one finds them all, and sly - ly feasts up - on the

THE THIEVISH MOUSE.

prize. A thief there sure-ly is se-cre-ted some-where in the house." But Grand-pa-pa, (the wise old man) de-clared it was a Mouse.

Said he, "We'll get a trap, and then you soon will find I'm right, Just toast a bit of cheese and make all rea-dy for to -

THE THIEVISH MOUSE.

wrong. She tas - ted pie and cake, then seized the cheese with ea - ger

greed. A - las! the trap closed with a spring, and she was caught in - deed.

Now lit - tle Folks be - lieve me, when you do a wick - ed

thing, Some - time or o - ther it is sure, its pun - ish - ment to

THE THIEVISH MOUSE.

bring, And no - thing can be worse you know, in peo - ple small or

grown, Than that of ta - king a - ny-thing which is not quite their own.

You see, if Mouse had stay'd at home, nor cared to pry and

peep, And had not trot - ted out to steal, while o - thers were a

THE THIEVISH MOUSE.

Marcato.

-sleep, She'd now have been a - live and well, and hap-py with her

friends, In - stead of be - ing caught and kill'd, to prove how steal-ing ends.

Dover Popular Songbooks

(Arranged by title)

ALEXANDER'S RAGTIME BAND AND OTHER FAVORITE SONG HITS, 1901–1911, David A. Jasen (ed.). Fifty vintage popular songs America still sings, reprinted in their entirety from the original editions. Introduction. 224pp. 9 x 12. (Available in U.S. only) 25331-7

AMERICAN BALLADS AND FOLK SONGS, John A. Lomax and Alan Lomax. Over 200 songs, music and lyrics: "Frankie and Albert," "John Henry," "Frog Went a-Courtin'," "Down in the Valley," "Skip to My Lou," other favorites. Notes on each song. 672pp. 5⅜ x 8½. 28276-7

AMERICAN FOLK SONGS FOR GUITAR, David Nadal (ed.). Forty-nine classics for beginning and intermediate guitar players, including "Beautiful Dreamer," "Amazing Grace," "Aura Lee," "John Henry," "The Gift to Be Simple," "Go Down, Moses," "Sweet Betsy from Pike," "Short'nin Bread," many more. 96pp. 9 x 12. 41700-X

THE AMERICAN SONG TREASURY: 100 Favorites, Theodore Raph (ed.). Complete piano arrangements, guitar chords, and lyrics for 100 best-loved tunes, "Buffalo Gals," "Oh, Suzanna," "Clementine," "Camptown Races," and much more. 416pp. 8¼ x 11. 25222-1

"BEALE STREET" AND OTHER CLASSIC BLUES: 38 Works, 1901–1921, David A. Jasen (ed.). "St. Louis Blues," "The Hesitating Blues," "Down Home Blues," "Jelly Roll Blues," "Railroad Blues," and many more. Reproduced directly from rare sheet music (including original covers). Introduction. 160pp. 9 x 12. (Available in U.S. only) 40183-9

THE CIVIL WAR SONGBOOK, Richard Crawford (ed.). 37 songs: "Battle Hymn of the Republic," "Drummer Boy of Shiloh," "Dixie," and 34 more. 157pp. 9 x 12. 23422-3

CIVIL WAR SONGS AND BALLADS FOR GUITAR, Compiled, Edited, and Arranged by Jerry Silverman. 41 favorites, among them "Marching Through Georgia," "The Battle Hymn of the Republic," "Tenting on the Old Camp Ground," and "When Johnny Comes Marching Home." 160pp. 9 x 12. 41902-9

FAVORITE CHRISTMAS CAROLS, selected and arranged by Charles J. F. Cofone. Title, music, first verse and refrain of 34 traditional carols in handsome calligraphy; also subsequent verses and other information in type. 79pp. 8⅜ x 11. 20445-6

FAVORITE SONGS OF THE NINETIES, Robert Fremont (ed.). 88 favorites: "Ta-Ra-Ra-Boom-De-Aye," "The Band Played on," "Bird in a Gilded Cage," etc. 401pp. 9 x 12. 21536-9

500 BEST-LOVED SONG LYRICS, Ronald Herder (ed.). Complete lyrics for well-known folk songs, hymns, popular and show tunes, more. "Oh Susanna," "The Battle Hymn of the Republic," "When Johnny Comes Marching Home," hundreds more. Indispensable for singalongs, parties, family get-togethers, etc. 416pp. 5⅜ x 8½. 29725-X

"FOR ME AND MY GAL" AND OTHER FAVORITE SONG HITS, 1915–1917, David A. Jasen (ed.). 31 great hits: Pretty Baby, MacNamara's Band, Over There, Old Grey Mare, Beale Street, M-O-T-H-E-R, more, with original sheet music covers, complete vocal and piano. 144pp. 9 x 12. 28127-2

MY FIRST BOOK OF AMERICAN FOLK SONGS: 20 Favorite Pieces in Easy Piano Arrangements, Bergerac (ed.). Expert settings of traditional favorites by a well-known composer and arranger for young pianists: *Amazing Grace, Blue Tail Fly, Sweet Betsy from Pike,* many more. 48pp. 8¼ x 11. 28885-4

MY FIRST BOOK OF CHRISTMAS SONGS: 20 Favorite Songs in Easy Piano Arrangements, Bergerac (ed.). Beginners will love playing these beloved favorites in easy arrangements: "Jingle Bells," "Deck the Halls," "Joy to the World," "Silent Night," "Away in a Manger," "Hark! The Herald Angels Sing," 14 more. Illustrations. 48pp. 8¼ x 11. 29718-7

ONE HUNDRED ENGLISH FOLKSONGS, Cecil J. Sharp (ed.). Border ballads, folksongs, collected from all over Great Britain. "Lord Bateman," "Henry Martin," "The Green Wedding," many others. Piano. 235pp. 9 x 12. 23192-5

"PEG O' MY HEART" AND OTHER FAVORITE SONG HITS, 1912 & 1913, Stanley Appelbaum (ed.). 36 songs by Berlin, Herbert, Handy and others, with complete lyrics, full piano arrangements and original sheet music covers in black and white. 176pp. 9 x 12. 25998-6

POPULAR IRISH SONGS, Florence Leniston (ed.). 37 all-time favorites with vocal and piano arrangements: "My Wild Irish Rose," "Irish Eyes are Smiling," "Last Rose of Summer," "Danny Boy," many more. 160pp. 26755-5

"A PRETTY GIRL IS LIKE A MELODY" AND OTHER FAVORITE SONG HITS, 1918–1919, David A. Jasen (ed.). "After You've Gone," "How Ya Gonna Keep 'Em Down on the Farm," "I'm Always Chasing Rainbows," "Rock-a-Bye Your Baby" and 36 other Golden Oldies. 176pp. 9 x 12. 29421-8

A RUSSIAN SONG BOOK, Rose N. Rubin and Michael Stillman (eds.). 25 traditional folk songs, plus 19 popular songs by twentieth-century composers. Full piano arrangements, guitar chords. Lyrics in original Cyrillic, transliteration and English translation. With discography. 112pp. 9 x 12. 26118-2

"THE ST. LOUIS BLUES" AND OTHER SONG HITS OF 1914, Sandy Marrone (ed.). Full vocal and piano for "By the Beautiful Sea," "Play a Simple Melody," "They Didn't Believe Me,"–21 songs in all. 112pp. 9 x 12. 26383-5

SEVENTY SCOTTISH SONGS, Helen Hopekirk (ed.). Complete piano and vocals for classics of Scottish song: *Flow Gently, Sweet Afton, Comin' thro' the Rye (Gin a Body Meet a Body), The Campbells are Comin', Robin Adair,* many more. 208pp. 8⅜ x 11. 27029-7

SONGS OF THE CIVIL WAR, Irwin Silber (ed.). Piano, vocal, guitar chords for 125 songs including "Battle Cry of Freedom," "Marching Through Georgia," "Dixie," "Oh, I'm a Good Old Rebel," "The Drummer Boy of Shiloh," many more. 400pp. 8⅜ x 11. 28438-7

STEPHEN FOSTER SONG BOOK, Stephen Foster. 40 favorites: "Beautiful Dreamer," "Camptown Races," "Jeanie with the Light Brown Hair," "My Old Kentucky Home," etc. 224pp. 9 x 12. 23048-1

"TAKE ME OUT TO THE BALL GAME" AND OTHER FAVORITE SONG HITS, 1906–1908, Lester Levy (ed.). 23 favorite songs from the turn-of-the-century with lyrics and original sheet music covers: "Cuddle Up a Little Closer, Lovey Mine," "Harrigan," "Shine on, Harvest Moon," "School Days," other hits. 128pp. 9 x 12. 24662-0

35 SONG HITS BY GREAT BLACK SONGWRITERS: Bert Williams, Eubie Blake, Ernest Hogan and Others, David A. Jasen (ed.). Ballads, show tunes, other early 20th-century works by black songwriters include "Some of These Days," "A Good Man Is Hard to Find," "I'm Just Wild About Harry," "Love Will Find a Way," 31 other classics. Reprinted from rare sheet music, original covers. 160pp. 9 x 12. (Available in U.S. only) 40416-1

*Available from your music dealer or write for **free** Music Catalog to*
Dover Publications, Inc., Dept. MUBI, 31 East 2nd Street, Mineola, NY 11501
*Visit us online at **www.doverpublications.com***